Praise for *Meet Your Muse*

Part memoir, part guidance, part invitation, this beautiful book provides an inspirational map to access your creative muse. Powerful lessons are distilled down to an essence as the authors expertly lead us through a process of becoming more creatively authentic. *Meet Your Muse* is a work of deep wisdom woven through an artist's touch and a dance of words. Deeply inspiring and joyfully captivating. What a gift!

Jeneen Piccuirro
Multi-passionate artist, founder of
Soul Voyage Studio

Meet Your Muse is a gentle companion and supportive guide for getting to know and trust the creativity that already dwells within you. I thoroughly enjoyed the book. I especially liked that it did not pressure the reader; it felt like a loving invitation. It is unique in its self-coaching approach—with inviting opportunities to explore and practice being in relationship with your creative nature. If you long for more creative expression in your life, *Meet Your Muse* is a perfect choice.

Laurie Mattila
Discovery Writing Instructor

Charise and Kathleen's generous sharing of their inner thoughts, emotions, and processes helped me understand how to use my mind, spirit, emotions, and physical body to express myself in words, art, and dance. Meeting my muse has sparked a renewed creative spark in my daily life.

Lucinda LaRee
Fitness Entrepreneur, CirqularX365 Creator/
Lifestyle Guide

To my mother, Dorothy, who told me that if you believe strongly enough in something, it can happen.

~Charise

To the life force Spirit who kindles the eternal fire of my creativity.

~Kate

ACKNOWLEDGMENTS

Grateful acknowledgment goes to Jeff Kaplan, our instructor for MentorCoach. We met through his coaching class and first began to work together in designing and presenting a virtual workshop titled "Meet Your Muse: Kindle Your Creativity." We thank Jeff for providing the spark and the support for our combined creative endeavors. The workshop evolved into writing *www.meetyourmuseblog.com*, which has culminated in the publication of this book.

Gratitude goes to Jo Parfitt, our publisher, who supported us in bringing *Meet Your Muse: The Dance of Creativity* to fruition.

Our thanks go to the authors, creatives, and spiritual teachers who have inspired and mentored us along the way.

CONTENTS

FOREWORD

It is my great pleasure to introduce you to *Meet Your Muse: The Dance of Creativity*, a book that will help you tap into your creative self to improve every aspect of your life. The authors, Charise and Kate, are great models of coaches who walk their talk, putting ideas into action. This book is such a wonderful snapshot of the creative, joyful, and dedicated energy they both brought to their foundational coaching class in 2008.

Charise and Kate are truly kindred spirits, each possessing a unique set of talents and experiences that bring with them the perspective of an artist, dancer, professional coach, yoga and qigong instructor, psychologist, and social worker. Charise and Kate share their stories and creative writings along with the wisdom of many other great authors, poets, musicians, and spiritual leaders.

Meet Your Muse is not just a book, it is an invitation to embark on a transformative journey of self-discovery and self-expression. Through personal narratives, thought-provoking questions, and practical exercises, the authors guide you on a path toward unlocking your true creative potential. As you engage with the book, you will discover that creativity is not just for the "artists," but is a natural part of your true nature.

What sets this book apart is the authors' ability to combine the concepts of Eastern philosophy, Greek mythology, and modern psychology to create a holistic approach to creativity. They encourage you to slow down and reflect on each component, to take time with each question, and to write your responses in the spaces provided. The result is a deep and meaningful exploration of your innermost self.

A book about creativity would be incomplete without visuals that enhance the writing. Charise and Kate do not disappoint as they pepper each chapter with beautiful drawings and pictures that taken in isolation could themselves lead to an in-depth exploration of one's creative mind.

I wholeheartedly recommend this book to anyone seeking to enhance their life and express their unique spirit. Whether you are a student, an artist, a business person, or simply someone looking to live a more fulfilling life, *Meet Your Muse* will help you tap into your creative spirit to enhance all aspects of your life. I am grateful to know the authors who poured their hearts and souls into this book to help their readers awaken the creative spirit within them.

Warmly,

Jeff Kaplan, PhD, MBA, MCC
President & CEO, Leading with Heart
Author of *The Anatomy of Habit Change: A Complete Dissection of Habits and How to Change Them*

INTRODUCTION

Creativity is part of your true nature—it is who you are. You are already creating in countless ways, in an evolving expression of yourself. You do not need to be a fine artist to be a maker of your life.

Everyone has a creative aspect to their being in the same way that they have a spiritual nature. You can cultivate a relationship with this part of you in order to enhance your life and express your unique spirit. Just as you might develop your spirituality through various practices, you also can develop your creativity. It lies within you, a mystery of life force energy, and awaits your active engagement in order to be expressed through you. We invite you to claim, cultivate, and celebrate your innate creativity.

The Muses are nine goddesses that govern the arts and sciences in Greek mythology. The nine girls cover all aspects of creativity, each inspiring a different expression. However, the word Muse can be defined in a way that resonates for you and relates to the life you are creating.

When we say, "*Meet Your Muse,*" we are talking about developing an intimate relationship with your creative nature. Intimacy means being attentive, caring, trusting, and responsive. When you get intimate with your Muse, this will, in turn, fuel your life and your work.

As you engage with your Muse, as with any relationship, you experience a rhythm of receiving and responding, much like in a dance. In our personal narratives, you will find a few literal examples of dance as an art form or a practice. Figuratively speaking, *"The Dance of Creativity"* is an active, spontaneous, harmonious relationship with your Muse. In that sense, dance is an expression of engagement. No one actually dances, but there is a sense of something happening that is dance-like—a joining, a connection—where you feel swept into the moment.

Who We Are

We are Charise and Kate: kindred spirits living very different lives. Between the two of us, we are artists, dancers, creativity coaches, yoga and qigong instructors, trained psychologists and social workers, writers, and healing arts practitioners. We met virtually in a coaching course in 2008, and quickly developed a synergy of thinking and writing about creativity. And, for 12 years, we have written the *Meet Your Muse* blog. It has been a monthly invitation to explore, expound, express, shape, cajole, and roll with the creative spirit that lives in all of us. Now we offer this book as a standing invitation for you to engage in the dance of creativity. We share our unique art expressions throughout the book: poetry, drawings, and watercolors.

HOW TO USE THIS BOOK

The book's five chapters explore the following five components of living a creative life:

BEING

    IN RELATIONSHIP

        WITH

           YOUR

               CREATIVE NATURE

We invite you to engage with your creative spirit as you slow down to reflect on each component. Take time with each one. You may want a separate journal to note your responses to the questions we ask, or you can write directly in the book in the spaces provided for this purpose in each chapter and at the end of the book. You can think about a question and then write a response later. There is no hurry; there is no right or wrong answer. When we suggest actions to take within each chapter, you can decide the best timeframe for you. You may want to spend a couple of weeks focused on one action, for example. Set your own pace. Developing and deepening your relationship with your creative nature includes both inner work and rest, in tandem with effort and expression.

You are already wired for creativity. Our hope is that you will experience this book beyond reading the words. We offer some information, concepts, and different ways for you to step into the dance of creativity. Your journey unfolds each time you take 'Your Turn.'

So, let's begin to *Meet Your Muse...*

1

BEING

Essence ~ Energy ~ Endless ~ Expansive

Creativity is an endless, renewable resource, your human potential, a treasure within. Yet few claim the ability to touch the living pulse of creativity; this seems to be left for 'artists.' As a maker of your life, you are an artist.

> *"From my point of view, your life is already artful—*
> *waiting, just waiting, for you to make it art."*
> —Toni Morrison, Princeton University lecture, 2005

The Essence of Creativity is Energy

Eastern thought views the foundation of all existence as pure energy. This perspective helps illuminate the very essence of creativity. One way to understand creative energy is through the lens of Tao, which is an underlying principle of the universe in Eastern thought. You may be familiar with the book *The Tao of Pooh*, which shows how this principle can be simply and playfully lived. Tao holds the complementary forces of yin and yang, experienced as light and dark, feminine and masculine. This is depicted in a unified circle containing the whole, Tao.

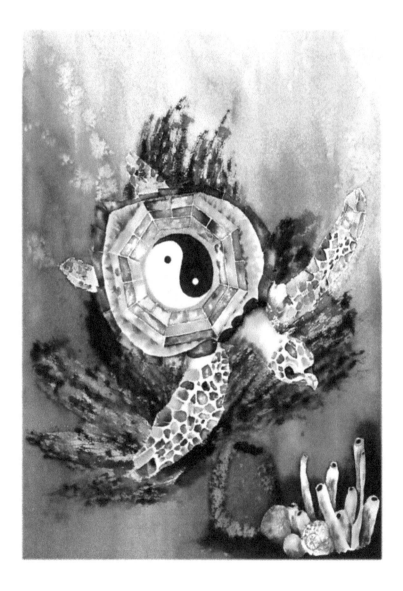

Tao Te Ching, written by Lao Tzu in the third century BCE, is considered to be the fundamental text of this Chinese philosophy. Tao, literally meaning 'the path' or 'the way' or 'flow of the universe,' is at the heart of this ancient text.

"The Way is to man as rivers and lakes are to fish,
the natural condition of life."
—Chuang Tzu

Tao is a single, overarching way that is in harmony with the natural order and encompasses everything in the universe. In essence, it is without name or form. In the embodiment of it, each creature or object has its own manifestation of Tao. This is true for you as a life form, a human being.

Your being encompasses the totality of creative energy. You are a microcosm of the macro universal energy. A drop of water is in the ocean and the ocean is in every drop of water. Many drops take the shape of a wave and then return to the larger body of water. You hold life force energy within you while also being a part of the whole circle of life.

"The ultimate mystery is one's own self."
—Sammy Davis, Jr.

Be in the *not* know. Begin within the mystery of who you are. Move from that mystery; be that mystery in its infinite possibility of expression. Your creative growth exists in this space of possibilities. After all, your body is mostly space. In each cell, the neutrons, protons, and electrons are whirring around in the spacious cell membrane. In the cosmos, the planets and stars are minute compared to the space in which they exist. As the universe continues to expand, so you too are born to expand.

Along with your expansiveness, you hold a wisdom inside of you that can guide and shape your life and work. It is that which is holy within you. As you deepen into your inner peace, you can arrive at this place of stillness. Everything unique and beautiful grows out of a still point.

> *"At the still point of the turning world."*
> —T.S. Eliot, *The Four Quartets*

You dwell in the mystery that dwells in you—your being reflects and expresses this essence.

KATE'S TURN

My logo, pictured above, originated while in a meditation. A phrase came to me: "I house the Spirit that houses me." I envisioned a light within me and all around me. I worked with a graphic artist until this image came to be my professional logo; it represents how I as much dwell in mystery as mystery dwells in me. The graphic artist said that this logo would lead me into the future. His words proved to be so true. The logo was first created for my Energy Psychology practice over 30 years ago. As my work evolved, it became fitting when I qualified as a qigong instructor. My teacher, Master Chunyi Lin, structures the qigong practice with three phrases that echo how the life force energy is within me and all around me.

Later in its evolution, my logo continued to be true in its representation as a creativity life coach. It was even the image on the spinnaker of my sailboat, Soul Dance, and now it's the image for my watercolor art signature. The truth of this phrase is the underlying current of all the different expressions that have grown out of the mystery within me. The logo's relevance in its many evolving applications speaks to its infinite depth and authentic truth as I have embodied and expressed this essence of mystery within.

Kate's story may spark a recollection or awareness of your own.

YOUR TURN

It is your turn to write your responses below the following questions as you begin to meet your Muse.

How do you connect with the life force energy within you and all around you?

Examples may be: gazing at the star-studded night sky, being in the presence of a newborn baby, viewing the beauty of a landscape, getting an inspiration that seems to come out of nowhere.

How do you experience mystery?

Let yourself live this question, contemplate on it, carry it around with you and enter its expanse. Note your insights.

"*I am in the Universe.*"
—Master Chunyi Lin, Qigong teacher
www.springforestqigong.com

This is the first declaration of his gentle movement practice.

Evoke ~ Embrace ~ Embody ~ Experience

Embrace and Experience the Energy of Creativity

Another relevant principle in Eastern thought is Te. Te is in a dynamic relationship with Tao. Tao is the natural condition of the flow of life. Te is the natural condition you are born with. It is like a template you have, awakened and nurtured by Tao, the flow of energy. Te is your embodiment of this energy while Tao is the essence of energy.

Every creation, every life, reflects this mysterious transformation of formless energy into manifestation of form. Through the process of creating, you experience the power, vitality, and vastness of Tao. Thus, your energy is connected to a greater energy that comes *through* you, not *from* you. You embrace Spirit as you move in the current of its river.

Your true nature is like a seed that experiences growth and expansion through nurturing. Your true nature radiates heart-light. Think of heart-light as the inner flame of Tao; your reception of this energy is the Te that shines through you in the unique expression of your being.

It is as if you are poised to evoke the Muse. You are ready. Here are examples of this readiness expressed in nature:

* Consider the womb. It is a space, a place of nurturing, a feminine embrace for the seed of new life.

* Picture fertile ground. It too is a receptacle ready to germinate a seed and help it mature into its true nature.

* Know that lightning always seeks to be grounded. Listen to your wildness, this raw energy, and have a readiness to receive it and give it form in your unique expression.

"Wildness we might consider as the root of the authentic spontaneities of any being. It is that wellspring of creativity whence comes the instinctive activities that enable all living beings to obtain their food, to find shelter, to bring forth their young: to sing and dance and fly through the air and swim through the depths of the sea. This is the same inner tendency that evokes the insight of the poet, the skill of the artist and the power of the shaman."

—Thomas Berry, *The Great Work: Our Way into the Future*

CHARISE'S TURN

Creativity is something I experience as movement. The end result isn't necessarily a movement form, such as dance. But there are parallels to dance: an empty studio or stage is a mirror of inner emptiness; the body moving represents the human embodiment of an inner impulse. There's a need for space, and a need for flow. That's a pretty basic formula for invoking the Muse. It can be easy to say that there isn't enough time, that my schedule is too full. But fullness is really about space. If I become too crowded with concerns about getting things done, or not getting things done, this becomes self-defeating.

In a daily routine, there are pockets of space to dip into. On a literal level, I experience this phenomenon during a bath (showers also work well in this regard). My mind is unencumbered, and therefore more spacious, in these moments of basic self-care. The water element supports flow. What tends to happen is this: a phrase or two that kickstarts a poem will float through. More work and crafting will follow at my laptop, but the Muse gift has been received.

YOUR TURN

What is your internal readiness for the evocation of the Muse?

Notice your anticipation for creative inspirations. Write down any practices that help you receive them.

How do you experience what Thomas Berry calls the "wellspring of creativity"?

Name ways that creative energy is expressed in your own unique style.

"The Universe is in my body."
—Master Chunyi Lin
This is the second declaration of his qigong practice.

Call to Creativity

"Creativity is a voice that calls us from dreams, that peeks out the corners of our eyes when we think no one is looking, the longing that breaks our hearts even when we think we should be happiest and to which we cannot give a name. When I was young, I heard the voice, the ticking, had the dream, but I didn't know what it was and felt only the pain, the longing that the voice inside brought me."
—Judy Collins, *Morning, Noon, and Night*

As Judy Collins says, "we cannot give a name" to that voice of creativity within you. It is the Voice before the voice, before the word, before the song, before the expression. Before the understanding that something wants expression. Like a tug, a calling, a rumbling, there is something going on internally, a certain energy. This energy is formless, and that's the beauty of it. It can take on any form and it can be restless, looking for a way to break through.

YOUR TURN

Consider your being as a significant embodiment of Being.

Pay attention to any internal signs of the voice of creativity within you. Some examples are: a word or phrase that delights you, an image or vision that fascinates you, a pattern that you find compelling. Name or draw your own examples.

"The Universe and I combine together."
—Master Chunyi Lin
This is the third declaration of his qigong practice.

2
BEING
IN RELATIONSHIP

Centering ~ Clearing ~ Commitment

The dynamic of your relationship with creativity is comprised of two aspects: *being* and *doing*. *Being* is the inner essence that you hold. It is a well that you tap into. *Doing* is the expression of this energy.

Being – Inner purpose – Tao

Doing – Outer purpose – Te

*"Your life has an inner purpose and an outer purpose. Inner
purpose concerns Being and is primary. Outer purpose concerns
doing and it is secondary... Your outer purpose can change
over time. It varies greatly from person to person. Finding and
living in alignment with the inner purpose is the foundation for
fulfilling your outer purpose. It is the basis for true success.
Without that alignment, you can still achieve certain things
through effort, struggle, determination, and sheer hard work or
cunning. But there is no joy in such endeavor, and it
invariably ends in some form of suffering."*
—Eckhart Tolle, *A New Earth*

Centering

You will be more able to respond to your Muse if you are centered. She does not impose; she invites. Through centering, you are more able to receive the present of the Present.

Creativity takes time… and then again… it doesn't! An inspiration happens in a nanosecond. A flash of an idea may appear on a walk, in the shower, while preparing a meal. Following up on that idea with creative expression takes time and focus, and a willingness to see where it takes you. Cultivating your creativity requires a conscious commitment to slowing down, staying aware of opportunistic moments, and allowing space and time for the creative process to take hold.

How to be most ready to receive

Value taking time to stay in touch with life's processes rather than getting swept up by productivity and outcome. For example, an architect friend of Kate creates pencil drawings instead of using computer models for his designs. He aspires to be a member of the Lead Pencil Society, whose motto is "Not so fast." Another example is the Cloud Appreciation Society, whose purpose is to return dignity to the art of loafing. Being idle can be something to aspire toward rather than reject. Cultivating the value of taking time results in an abundant manifestation of creativity.

"Niksen is… great for our creativity because it gives time for our thoughts to wander, which results in insights that we may have not come up with otherwise."
—Olga Mecking, Niksen:
Embracing the Dutch Art of Doing Nothing

CHARISE'S TURN

The sunroom of my house is a great place to hang out—the walls are painted teal and there are windows wrapping around three sides. At different times of the day, the light shifts. I go there when I need a break from work or routine. There's no agenda, and my cat often joins me. Basically, I relax, and in that space of relaxation, my mind drifts.

Here is a poem I crafted based on my sunroom breaks. I put together five stanzas of haikus with a smattering of rhyme to create a rhythm, sound, and vocabulary that heightens an experience of slowing down.

Rest Assured

To the nothingness
of an absent gaze absorbed
in daydreams, raptness

To lollygagging,
lax within solarium
room of rays slanting

To the stalled answer,
not lacking for repartee,
but loathe to capture

To the waste of time,
dilly-dally from the more
makings to call mine

To the scrape of aim
that drags: a sunken seed will
bring the newly named

—Charise M. Hoge

YOUR TURN

How could you devote some time to what you really value in your heart?

Draw your own clouds, filling in what you value, similar to our examples.

Engaging with loved ones...

Committing to quiet time to offer balance for yourself...

Spending some idle time watching clouds pass...

How to be most aligned

You feel spacious and free when you experience alignment because nothing is tugging out of place or lacking in your awareness. A spacious, free, aware feeling can be a metric for decisions and choices in your life. When a decision is merely arbitrary, it is like going through the motions in a half-hearted way. When your actions are not in alignment with your *being*, there is a harming effect in the same way physical mis-alignment can lead to injury. When a decision settles in your being like a welcome sigh—like a tap opening to a deeper wellspring—there is an enlivening effect. Then you know you are aligning with your inner purpose.

"Where talents and the needs of the world cross,
therein lies your vocation."
—Aristotle

To have a vision for your creative expression, meaningful work, or fulfilled life is not necessarily some lofty or laborious process. Rather, it is a matter of paying attention and setting intention. Your vision is generated from your wellspring within. The possibilities and variations are infinite.

Imagine a crossroad:

* The vertical axis holds what you love and are passionate about in your heart, inspired by the imagination of
  your mind (heart-mind).

* The horizontal axis carries your expression externally
  through your hands.

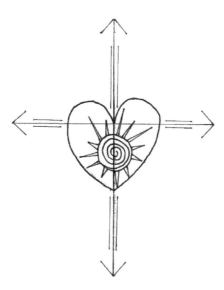

This crossroad can lead to many roads. Just imagine, if you
will, what your journey would be like if you truly allowed your
heart-mind to lead you in a conscious, mindful way.

When you pay attention to your movement forward in life, from where in your body do you initiate your next step? "Obviously," you say, "with my foot." Well, yes, the foot does have to move forward. But if you back up a bit in your perspective, you may realize that you move from your intention, and that intention originates from your center, consciously or unconsciously.

A labyrinth is a path, created usually in a round shape, with a series of concentric paths, that twist and turn, until you find yourself in the center… and then, from that center, you walk the return path to depart. It may look like a maze, but is different, in that a maze has many dead ends that force you to back up and try again to find the path through. A labyrinth has only one direction leading to the center, and one direction leading out. Labyrinths date back centuries. They are found in many areas of the world and have more recently become popular as sacred sites for ceremony and spiritual renewal.

Walking a labyrinth offers a time to reflect on how you walk through life, with all its twists and turns. Arriving at the center offers a chance to release what no longer serves you. You can open yourself to healing energy and renew your continued journey back out into life. Each step, led by your heart's desires and by what you know to be true in your gut, can add up to a lifetime of steps that bring fulfillment and satisfaction. Your own center is your compass that guides you in consciously creating your life, moment by moment.

YOUR TURN

Practice, if only for a minute or two, walking mindfully, leading from your center, moment by moment.

In addition, you may wish to trace with your finger this labyrinth image or walk one that is full-scale in your community.

Name some times that you have already experienced being led from your heart-mind center.

Examples: being compelled to act, trusting your intuition.

How is your Muse inviting you to step forward from your center rather than being deterred by distractions?

Consider what intentions you have that are asking for your attention. Note them here.

Clearing

Clearing is a term that refers to making the space for the best possible outcome. That space supports you to be receptive, open, and prepared to take steps forward.

How to be most receptive

You may have heard of *The Artist's Way* by Julia Cameron and the technique of Morning Pages: writing when you first wake up without correcting, without stopping, emptying thoughts and feelings on paper. It is basically a dump. It clears the chatter of your mind—the daily data, if you will—and allows you to access what is not readily apparent but wants to be known.

> *"Learn to free yourself from all things that have molded you*
> *And which limit your secret and undiscovered road."*
> —Ben Okri, Nigerian poet

After you set an intention to express creatively, you then act; you take steps to carry out your idea. Often, that is when the parameters, the hidden restrictions, begin to show themselves.

The Knots Prayer

Dear God:
Please untie the knots
that are in my mind,
my heart, and my life.
Remove the have nots,
the can nots and the do nots
that I have in my mind.

Erase the will nots, may nots
might nots that may find
a home in my heart.

Release me from the could nots,
would nots and should nots
that obstruct my life.

And most of all, Dear God,
I ask that you remove from my mind,
my heart, and my life all the am nots
that I have allowed to hold me back,
especially the thought
that I am not good enough.
Amen.

—Anonymous poet from South Africa

CHARISE'S TURN

With good intentions, I purchased the book *The Artist's Way* when my youngest daughter was six years old. As soon as I read about the Morning Pages, in a section titled "The Basic Tools," I became totally disheartened. My mornings began with the demands of taking care of a family. It wasn't possible to have the privacy or quiet needed to write three pages after waking up. Not once did it occur to me to adapt the practice to my own life. I only considered how the ideal structure was not going to work, how it was not feasible, not realistic. The flip side of these 'not' roadblocks is the consideration of what is possible. And I have found a way to become devoted to writing, with all its messy and amusing starts, just like Morning Pages. But it doesn't happen first thing in the morning. It's kind of happening all the time, at least in the sense of believing in the power of writing and looking for an opportune time to jot things down. I end up surprising myself with what shows up on the page. And the excitement around this surprise motivates me to keep at it, to make a new start again and again.

YOUR TURN

Clearing is simple. Experiment with these different methods.

Say to yourself "okay" and breathe quietly for a few moments.

Bring your hands together in prayer fashion and set your intention.

Light a candle to bless the moment.

These are all rituals that put import on what you are doing and that honor the impact your actions have.

"When clutches of the 'self' break away, they clap their hands and break into dance as their imperfections fade away. The musicians within strike the tambourine, and the seas burst into foam at their ecstasy."
—Rumi

How to be most open

In order to move forward, you have to let go of the past. This preparation clears a space in which you are free to expand. If you're stuck in what used to be, then you have no room for what could be, for what you want.

*"We must be willing to get rid of the life we've planned,
so as to have the life that is waiting for us."*
—Joseph Campbell, mythology scholar

Clearing what is no longer fresh and alive serves your readiness for new expansion and growth. It seems that people gravitate toward filling up whatever space they have, whatever seems to be empty, whether it is a closet, time, conversation, silence, and so on. Embrace this emptiness in anticipation of future expansion.

YOUR TURN

What areas in your life call for more space?

Some examples are: a shelf, a drawer, a negative belief, a limitation that is choking growth, an unwillingness, an inner resistance. Identify yours.

Foyer

Rather than an exposé
on entryways
—another excuse
to look askance
at polished wood
purporting to be a drawer
of a console table
whose contents are known—
you entreat me to explore
the depths of neglect,
and leave the budding poem
at the door.

—Charise M. Hoge, published in "Next Line, Please"
(10/17/2017), *The American Scholar*

When you root out mindsets that inhibit change, you open space for greater expansion of yourself. An image that comes to mind is a pregnant mother, making ready a nursery space in which to nurture her child, anticipating the possibilities for the wonder of its growth and becoming. This is an image you can embody in your readiness for new life. It is in the spirit of this readiness, along with anticipation of the new life to come, that you can clear and open the space, ready to receive. Visualize your newly opened space as a creative incubator, holding the space open to embrace what is waiting to emerge. This is the birthplace of manifestation.

"We must live in this world and be gardens for
the dreams that want to take root in it."
—Robert Moss, *Dreaming True*

Actions that sabotage your intention act like weeds in a garden—starting small and spreading quickly, choking out the intended blossoming. You can reassess the choices you are making that are reflected in the 'garden' that you are.

KATE'S TURN

Currently, my own creative space is too cluttered. I have too many projects in front of me, along with the materials needed for them. It reminds me of a flower garden that has spread over time, such that plantings have taken over other areas. I believe the environment needs to be conducive to growth. My space needs some clearing. And having more organization and prioritization will help me focus more effectively.

I have also realized that I finally get to my creative projects once my other life tasks are taken care of, if I have the time. This belief is choking my creative expression. I prefer to give my creative expression space by changing this belief from 'if I have time' to 'taking the time' so I can enjoy this space as part of my lifestyle rather than as a maybe-add-on. This means prioritizing consistent times to play in my creative space and leaving less urgent life tasks until later, if I have time.

These two modifications will enrich my creative expression.

CHARISE'S TURN

I have used the garden template on the next page as a visual tool to understand how I develop creative work, and it is apparent that clearing, centering, and commitment are all over the map. Both the weeds and the overgrowth are areas to clear. For me, these relate to overwhelm. It's easy for me to feel overwhelmed at the prospect of attending to my art (poetry) when life is constantly in flux. Here's something I've learned to do: ignore the weeds/overgrowth. In other words, let the overwhelm have its place and shift my attention to the art. It's a different type of clearing than weeding... an indirect approach to minimizing the weeds. My overwhelm doesn't get a chance to usurp the creative impulse of my spirit.

Another aspect of the template, the stepping stones, suggest a movement of commitment. What I need between each stone is a pause for centering. One step is such a huge step, and to do that I have to kind of catch my breath before taking another... to check in and make sure the one I've just taken feels right. Maybe a visit to the mature growth area is warranted, a sidestep. That's where my completed projects (books, for example), or completed portions of projects, show what is being nurtured... both within myself and for others. Maybe a little dreaming needs to happen (dream seeds) before something more definitive can take shape. It's reassuring to me to realize that no matter what is going on or where my focus lands, I'm carrying around a garden that wants to come to life.

YOUR TURN

Begin to fill in the garden of your dreams using the template below, naming your seeds, sprouts, weeds, stepping stones, mature growth, and overgrowth.

Seeds are ideas you have in mind, sprouts are projects that you have just begun, weeds are obstacles, stepping stones are plans, mature growth is accomplishment, overgrowth is clutter.

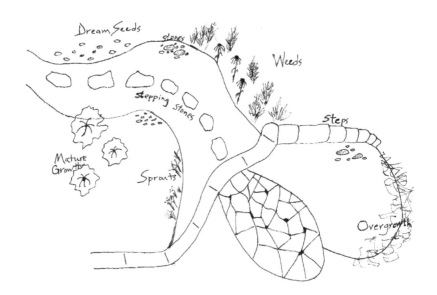

How to take steps forward

Taking new steps moves you into unknown territory, which can feel scary or risky. What if you approach this as a learning experience rather than a perfected performance? Fear often has the upper hand by paralyzing you into non-action. When you ease the tension between your fear and a hunch to move forward, you can listen to the something that creativity is trying to tell you.

You can use the following mindset to sidestep your fear: "Let's just try this and see what happens." When you feel clear, you are free to step into something new. This is the 'aha!' moment that calls you forward.

YOUR TURN

What do you need to do in order to take your next step?

Choose a way to get clear before you take action. Identify any mindset that stops you in your tracks.

Even if you feel fear, follow your hunch. Be open to trying new things even when results are uncertain. You will have the opportunity to respond to unexpected results and learn from them. In fact, this is how your life has evolved.

"The price of inaction is far greater than the cost
of making a mistake."
—Meister Eckhart, 14th-century German mystic

Commitment

Commitment is the first movement in the dance of co-creating. When you are centered and clear, it is time to say "Yes" in your relationship with creativity. Then your creative manifestations will unfold.

"The moment one definitely commits oneself, then Providence moves
too. All sorts of things occur to help one that would never have
otherwise occurred... unforeseen incidents and meetings and
material assistance, which no man could have dreamed
would have come his way."
—W.H. Murray, *The Scottish Himalayan Expedition*

KATE'S TURN

One of the times I experienced Providence was during our transition from living aboard our sailboat to moving back to land life. On our final sail from Venezuela to the US Virgin Islands, I asked the universe for an energy-healing community and an artists' community to connect with. I was anticipating letting go of the limitless adventure journey I had experienced for eight years. How could I go from exploring endless horizons to confining my world to an apartment? I thought finding communities in spirituality and creativity would help ease this shift. And that is exactly how Providence moved on my behalf. Once I made that commitment to go forward in my life, and I put that prayer out into the universe, after only a week, I found that I was welcomed into both of these types of communities. I met with a group of artists every Friday to paint plein air on a different part of St. Croix. And some of those artists became my teachers over the next five years, helping me develop my craft. Also, after having my own personal practice of qigong for ten years, I became certified as an instructor. I taught qigong classes on the island and participated in other spiritual energy healing events as well. Even though it felt like magic to be ushered into these communities so quickly, I believe that my intention, openness, and commitment allowed me to experience the floodgates opening on my behalf.

YOUR TURN

Use this simple practice to affirm your readiness to commit to being in relationship with creativity:

Place the palm of one hand on the center of your forehead over the third eye.

Affirm three times, "I am clear."

Take a deep breath in, and let it out with a sigh.

Now move your hand and place it over your heart.

Affirm three times, "I am here."

3

BEING
IN RELATIONSHIP
WITH

*Working the Magic ~ Wildness, Grounded & Expressed ~
Welcoming the Dance*

The creative force flows through you, anchored within your unique spirit. This makes for a lifetime of unfolding, blooming, shining, dancing.

WITH is a dance of co-creating

It is a dynamic of your passion – your desire – your intention

engaging in relationship *WITH*

Force energy that you embody – a deeper impulse – a larger
energy within you

*"We rarely hear the inward music,
but we're all dancing to it nevertheless."*
—Rumi

So, who is leading this dance? It is a synergistic partnering. When you meet your Muse, you make contact with a divine spark within your creative self. You a-Muse, engage, and experiment with it. You kindle that divine flame into an expression of your heart, your heart-light.

Working the Magic

Subtle, seemingly silent energies are available to you as you honor both your inner passion and the outer influences of your creative expression. These energies are like angels, in that they are always available to help you carry out your creative expression, if you are open to entertain them in your process. When you release an attachment to a specific outcome, you create space for these energies to exponentially expand your expression. Stay open as you honor your process so that these forces can influence the final work. When they show up in the creative process it may seem like a miracle; it can feel magical.

"For original ideas to come about, you have to let them percolate under the level of consciousness in a place where we have no way to make them obey our own desires or our own direction. So, they find their way, their random combinations that are driven by forces we don't know about. It's through this recombination that something new may come up, not when we try to push them directly."
—Mihaly Csikszentmihalyi, interviewed by Michael Toms,
New Dimensions newsletter

KATE'S TURN

My earlier watercolor paintings tend to be photorealistic. One of the first times I used artistic license for a more original watercolor painting was the turtle labyrinth you saw in *Chapter 2*. I love swimming with sea turtles. They symbolize an ancient spiritual wisdom for me. The hunch that persisted and percolated in this composition was to pattern the back of the turtle shell with a labyrinth. Even against my resistance to this idea—turtle shells don't have labyrinths on them—I felt compelled to give my hunch a try. The mingling of colors and light in a labyrinth pattern resembles stained glass, which, by the way, I also love. All of these random desires combined to make this magical turtle. It has been my best seller by far at art fairs for it speaks to a universal story.

YOUR TURN

What hunch may be percolating beneath the surface for you?

Jot down any ideas that come to mind, especially those that bubble up more often.

"A hunch is creativity trying to tell you something."
—Frank Capra, American filmmaker

Perhaps as you are musing about new forms for your work, you may notice an urgency to just push forth and *make* something happen. It takes a lot of courage and patience to allow the inner creative force to play its part. "Trust in the slow work of God," says Pierre Teilhard de Chardin. The wiser part of you trusts that larger force within you to co-create, and to carry you to an outcome greater than you could ever imagine.

The word 'force' is both a verb and a noun. As a verb, force is an exerting of will and control toward a desired outcome. As a noun, force is the power or essence of the strength exerted. Force is yang energy: the masculine active principle, the effort you put forth in the creative process. Simultaneously, you activate yin energy: the feminine, receiving aspect, the embrace of your Muse. This interplay is the dance of co-creating.

YOUR TURN

How do you cultivate conditions to allow the creative force to do its magic?

For example: pausing, contemplating, holding the space for further inspiration.

"Whatever you can do, or dream you can do, begin it.
Boldness has genius, power, and magic in it!"
—Johann Wolfgang von Goethe, Faust couplet

In your creative endeavor, you may run out of steam, or obstacles may arise that interfere with your progress. Limitations can often be advantageous to creativity. Consider the outpouring of innovation generated by the constraints of the global pandemic. Surrendering to what seems like a roadblock allows the percolation of creativity to present itself. It is a yin approach to a yang force. Both are essential to co-create. Look how new life emerges in the spring when the seed and soil yield to the force of the sun. Welcome this warming light as you surrender to the creative forces within and all around you.

"See how your soul is a sire of light."
—Hafiz, 14th-century Persian poet

YOUR TURN

Sit and breathe for a couple of minutes to access your creative source.

One way to open yourself to creative energy is with Ushas Mudra, a yoga hand position for creativity. This mudra is a simple act of interlacing the fingers of your hands and clasping them together. Stay with this mudra and focus on your breath for as long as you wish.

"By the expenditure of hope, intelligence, and work, you think you have it fixed. It is unfixed by rule. Within the darkness, all is being changed, and you also will be changed... and yet, and yet the light breaks in, heaven seizing its moments that are at once its own and yours."
—Wendell Berry, "Sabbath 1998, VI," Given: Poems

Wildness, Grounded & Expressed

Imaginations can run 'wild'; dreams are 'wild.' A popular phrase, 'beyond your wildest imagination,' is used when expectations have been exceeded. This can happen when you have an openness, a willingness, a readiness to respond to the Muse. Think of creativity as lightning being grounded, harnessing its wild power to affect a desired outcome. Listen to the wild and ride its power 'beyond your wildest imagination.'

KATE'S TURN

This phrase 'beyond my wildest imagination' has become a frequent expression in the unfolding of my life path. An early example is when I established my holistic psychology practice over 35 years ago; I was delighted and amazed that I could bring my whole self to my work. My training in psychology and spirituality are both integral in addressing issues of body, mind, and spirit. I had never imagined this coalescence and alignment when I was in graduate school. Another example is when I participated in a group study of *The Artist's Way* by Julia Cameron. The surprising outcome I created was an experiential presentation for a statewide spirituality conference. Again, I had never seen myself as a presenter, especially on such a large scale, and had no idea upon joining the group that I would be doing such an event. However, one of the wildest rides in my life was when I met my husband and, five years later, found myself on our sailboat, Soul Dance, heading south to the Caribbean. We both closed our respective businesses, pulled up the anchors of our land life, and lived aboard in the Caribbean for eight years. After selling our boat, we lived on an island for five years and both worked in new businesses that we had developed. I had become certified as a life coach, and also as a qigong instructor. In addition, I became a watercolor artist! I participated in many art shows, two of which were my own solo exhibits. After 13 years in the tropics, we returned from abroad to once more root ourselves in land life. My life had expanded and unfolded in ways that truly were 'beyond my wildest imagination!' In retrospect, I realize that co-creating with the Muse clearly is a dance that takes on a life of its own; I never know where it will take me. Any expectations I had have been exceeded by being open, ready, and willing to trust the Spirit of the dance.

YOUR TURN

Name an example that activated your imagination to the point of engagement.

For instance, you may remember a teacher whose use of imagination engaged you so effectively that you remember their lessons lifelong. Or you may have experienced being pulled into an advertisement through its appeal to your imagination, evoking a response in you at a primal level.

How can you use your imagination to partner with your Muse?

Name some wild ideas that you would like to entertain as possibilities.

How do you quiet yourself so that you listen to your wild?

Identify ways that you quiet your mind and tune in to your Muse. These can either be active, such as gardening or walking, or contemplative.

*"If waters are placid, the moon will be mirrored perfectly. If we still
ourselves, we can mirror the divine perfectly… There is no effort
that we can make to still ourselves. True stillness comes naturally
from moments of solitude where we allow our minds to settle…
Neither the water nor the moon make any effort
to achieve a reflection."*
—Deng Ming-Dao, 365 Tao: Daily Meditations

CHARISE'S TURN

I was drawn to yoga as a child, before classes were readily
available. PBS had a show called *Hatha Yoga with Kathleen
Hitchcock*, and I followed it, trying the poses in my parents'
bedroom. It was evident to me that this was different from my
ballet training and my gym class at school. There was an
organization of effort on a physical and mental level that fed
me internally, that did not aim toward performance. Yoga was
about settling into being.

Flash forward to my mid-30s, when my training as an
instructor of dance as a healing art (SynergyDance) included
a class called Still Motion. The appeal of movement that
instills a quiet aliveness was rekindled. As a mother of two

young daughters and supervisor of my own mother's care, I relished this experience that restored me to myself, or perhaps, more accurately, to my spirit. Subsequent yoga training permitted me to expand a spirit-led practice, both by teaching others and tending to my personal journey.

When I developed tinnitus a handful of years ago, I learned that a lack of quiet is not the same as a lack of stillness. Even with an ongoing sound that no one else can hear, I can relax into a deep silence that is not connected to the defects of the body. It doesn't take long, and it doesn't have to be for a long amount of time. I sit, do some breathwork, find communion with the essence of my existence. This helps tremendously with feeling cluttered internally with responsibilities and any accompanying sense of overwhelm. I know that everything goes more smoothly and spontaneously if I step back and tune in. Clarity exists here, in the stillness. It's just like the quote above: "If waters are placid, the moon will be mirrored perfectly."

YOUR TURN

Pay attention to your state of being as you go through your day.

Notice what happens as you: sit at your desk; attend to a task at hand; take a walk; engage with another person; prepare food; read; dabble; think about different things. Let a mindfulness accompany you all through the day and be curious about yourself. See where your energy flows and where your inner listening goes.

Experience this mode of awake rest.

Breathe in, breathe out.

Breathe in, let go as you breathe out.

Breathe in, let go as you breathe out and let in the effect of your inspiration.

Let in the effect of your inspiration.

Ready... let it in.

Use writing as a tool to channel your inspirations.

The word 'inspire' comes from the Latin *inspirare* which means to inhale. Your inhalation is an opening for your inspiration.

> *"Writing, to me, is simply thinking through my fingers."*
> —Isaac Asimov, American author

Begin writing about inspiration, using the following questions as a guide:

* How do your passions and desires connect with what you discover as you write?

* How do your values show up in this writing practice?

* How can you make writing a powerful tool to illuminate what you want to express?

You may not have answers right away. Reflect, carry the questions with you for a while, see what surfaces. Using 'how' in your inquiry will open you to the possibility of change. Knowing your 'how' gives you the know-how to succeed.

"It's on the strength of observation and reflection that one finds a way. So we must dig and delve unceasingly."
—Claude Monet, French painter

Welcoming the Dance

"But what I have learned in time, in 32 years of writing, is that it's a lot of work, and if I just show up, and I work and work, there is a moment, a magical moment, at some point, when it gives. And then you don't need the effort anymore. It's like dancing. When you're dancing and counting the steps, you're not dancing. When your body just goes—then you're dancing, and then there's a rhythm, there's a velocity, there's a feeling, there's a joy that you cannot describe. And it happens in spite of me. I think that's the moment in writing when the book starts to happen. From that point on, it's all joy. At the beginning, it's work."
—Isabel Allende, interviewed by Gabriel Packard for *The Writer Magazine*

The dance of co-creating is a partnership. You are not alone. When you partner *with* your Muse, you set in motion the dance that is inherent to being in relationship. This dance includes both the quieter energy of receptivity along with the active, expansive energy of expression. The give and take of that dance can be subtle. Imagine a quieter fire—one that draws in, one that welcomes the world to pull up a chair to your hearth, to your heart-light. And when you stoke that fire, it expands. You are partnering with these complementary energies as you welcome (yin) and express outwardly (yang) your creative spirit. You activate both yin and yang energy in the dance with creativity.

4

BEING IN RELATIONSHIP WITH YOUR

Focus~ Form ~ Fuel ~ Flow

Creativity is no more limited to the fine arts than spirituality is reserved for people of religious orders. You are not always mindful that you are expressing creatively, just like you are not always mindful of how you are breathing. Your eyes fall on what you love, and you immerse yourself in it. All along, you are cultivating your creative expression.

Focus on Your Part in the Dance of Creativity

How many of us are aware that we are creating all the time? We are probably doing so unconsciously. Life unfolds, takes unexpected turns; choices are made, consequences are felt. Staying connected to what you value in a life well lived will guide your actions to a result that satisfies.

"How you spend your days is how you spend your life."
—Annie Dillard, *The Writing Life*

Clarity of purpose allows you to root yourself in your being and blossom in your intention to be who you are. You not only intend to blossom—you choose to blossom. Each choice becomes a "Yes!" to your purpose. And each action strengthens a pattern, a habit that embodies as your character.

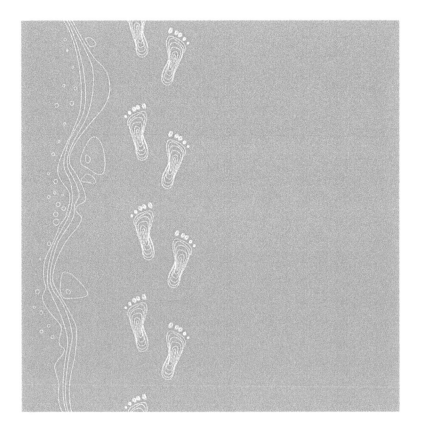

CHARISE'S TURN

My first website was *Coaching Moves.* The phrase refers to physical moves of dance or yoga as well as international moves of relocation. The logo, the brand, that I chose was an image of footprints along a shoreline. Perfect, but not mine! Lacking the skill of a visual artist, I had to borrow the thing that I could not create. When I purchased this image, however, I flipped it for a different orientation and also altered the color. You could say I put my stamp on it. And how about the fact that I knew what I was looking for? I love the spirals that fill the impression of the soles of the feet—it seems to slow down the movement of the steps. Spirals and steps, fluid and forward at the same time. Inward journey as well as travel is what this image represents for me. The meaning of the art belongs to my unique focus. My hope is that anyone engaging with this logo will see a path and will relate to the idea of being a path maker.

"Do not live in the shadow of the masters forever. Learn to live in the light of your soul. Life deserves full expression."
—Amit Ray, *Meditation*

Claim your artist within. Create a life that speaks to what is sacred in you. Shine your heart-light. Being true to your purpose opens the space that allows for an expression that delights and gratifies, and benefits others as well. Living out your purpose brings you happiness, like a river of joy moving through you.

*"When you do things from your soul,
you feel a river moving in you. A joy."*
—Rumi

YOUR TURN

How does each choice you make build your character?

Consider what kind of person you want to be as you create your life. Identify the choices that follow your intentions.

What is needed for you to blossom more fully?

We invite you to continue filling in your garden sketch that is in *Chapter 2*.

What 'weeds' of restriction need to be cleared to allow for your expression?

Add this to your garden sketch.

> *"Sow a thought and you reap an act;*
> *Sow an act and you reap a habit;*
> *Sow a habit and you reap a character;*
> *Sow a character and you reap a destiny."*
> —Samuel Smiles, British author

Say "Yes" to your intention to be who you are, to claim your uniqueness. You are already here as a unique being. Another way to say this is that *you are all ready here*. You are equipped with creative potential. And your uniqueness is essential to the expression of life on this earth.

KATE'S TURN

When I was a young adult, I never considered myself creative. Having a farm upbringing, I would more aptly describe myself as concrete and practical, externally referenced. After all, a recipe has a specific process to follow, and a math problem has one correct answer. In my thirties, when the job I wanted did not naturally follow from the education I had completed (linear thinking), I was thrown into a 'crisis.' My intention to be a family therapist was not being realized. Through a career counseling process, I came to realize that spirituality is one of my signature strengths and needs to be an integral part of my work. Thus, I shifted my focus and quickly found work as a pastoral counselor. And as my profession evolved, my private practice reflected a holistic approach, addressing body, mind, and spirit in the healing process. Resolution of this 'crisis' made me realize that there were numerous options for me to choose from for the trajectory of my career. I specifically remember my spiritual guide during this time teaching me how to express myself using metaphors when concrete, literal terms were not sufficient. What a world that opened for me! I also remember a psychic telling me I was extremely creative when I had yet to see myself that way. I was shocked and said, "I am?" But as I evolved in my profession, I gradually came to realize my creativity was manifesting in how I developed rapport and trust in the therapeutic relationship, how I assisted clients to meet their challenges, and even how I decorated my office space to reflect my own passions and interests.

I began to claim my creativity in *all* aspects of my life. I came to realize that my creativity is an innate resource that I draw upon when I make choices that shape my life. I have a whole host of options at every turn. I had uncovered a way to view myself that had been hidden previously by trying to find the right answer or do something the right way, such as looking outside myself, for instance. Instead, I was now shaping the course of my life from the inside out. I am, and always have been, already creative.

"In each individual the earth breaks its silence."
—John O'Donohue, Eternal Echoes

YOUR TURN

What are your top five signature strengths?

Discover what your signature strengths are and list them below.

You can take a survey at no cost at:
www.authentichappiness.org.

How are you already expressing creativity?

Your signature strengths give you clues to knowing your unique ways. Name them.

How are you using your essential voice to break earth's silence, as John O'Donohue suggests? How is your expression showing up and taking form?

Contemplating these questions stirs a deeper thinking about your unique sense of purpose. Then, from that place of deeper thinking, note your insights.

Form is Your Expression of the Creative Force Flowing Through You

You are a funnel to channel the creative force, and you actively funnel this energy into form through your expression. You are both receptive and active with the creative force. You embody this force as you embody creativity.

CHARISE'S TURN

An example of this embodiment happens in dance improvisation: you engage in an unfolding arm movement that is not a typical stretch or reach. You are moving through the joints, letting movement rise wave-like through shoulders, elbows, wrists, hands, fingers. This allows for sequencing, receptivity, and softness. It is the antithesis of grasping; it lends a quality of release, trust, and openness at a very intimate level with your own body-based beingness. You feel connected to a pulsation of life all the way through to the tips of your fingers.

KATE'S TURN

I have experienced sailing as an example of this dynamic of being both receptive and active with the forces of the winds. Choices are made all along that enable me to arrive at my destination. "We can't direct the wind, but we can adjust the sails" is a common saying that illustrates this. The wind blows as it will but I have a destination in mind, so we need to work together so I can harness its power toward my intended course. This is achieved through my actions taken at the helm, such as trimming the sails, staying on a particular course, and adjusting with the variations of the wind. The sails, channeling the forces of the wind, in concert with my actions at the helm, lead me in an unfolding dance of water and wind.

How you approach an endeavor or project is another way of saying how to bring your self to it. This is where you connect with what you are saying or creating; and when you connect, then others will too. The form funnels the vitality of your coming-into-the-creative-moment. The funnel is necessary, but it is empty without your pouring into it. Allow your spirit to move into the form of your creative expression. The beginning is a purposeful impulse or action which leads to a process of unfolding. Here are some examples: sign up for a class that appeals to you and draws you into fuller expression; pick up a pen and paper or turn on your electronic device to begin to write.

Writing is a tool to help formulate your ideas. As nature dictates, in order for something to flourish, it must take root first. Research has shown that when you write down your goals, they are much more likely to happen. Think of the action of writing—whatever is floating around in your thoughts takes form as words, so you are already taking the first step into the physical realm of manifestation. You are grounding your ideas. Right? Write!

YOUR TURN

Use these questions to write down how the creative force is flowing through you. Your responses can be playful, exploratory, and imaginative.

What would your life book title be?

What is the song you came to sing?

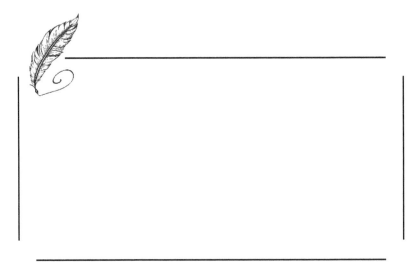

How are you dancing through life?

How are you the star of your own play?

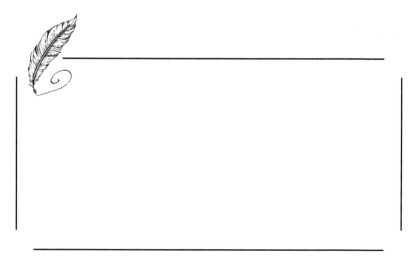

If your life were a painting, what mood would it convey, what beauty, what message?

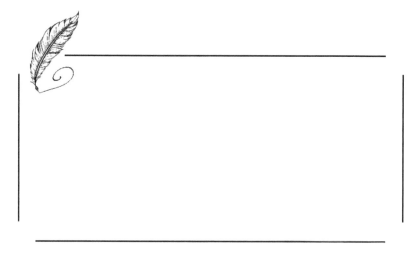

Fuel to Sustain Your Creative Effort

Sustainability is vital to a long-range plan of increasing output and preventing burnout. Farmers intentionally allow a piece of land to lie fallow, protecting it from the eventual depletion of its ability to be productive. Progressive corporations build in naps for their employees, recognizing that this period of rest is, in fact, a time of consolidation of ideas that contributes to innovative production.

Intervals of idleness are essential to creative work. Shakespeare, we are told, was habitually idle between plays. This non-productive time allows the subconscious to shine through. Great work is based on a connection with the creator's inner world, a place of both still and musing meditation.

Have a plan for downtime, a time to do nothing. This time of solitude acts as a period of recharging to avoid the risk of becoming depleted. Rest as if in a dark womb. Trust in the knowing that you will give birth to the sunlight in your being as you are receptive to Spirit in your still point. Elevate rest to an important place in your life.

Now Nothing

I hope you have the chance to do nothing.
You can stop here, heed no further.

Or nestle between beginnings/endings
of wording: there   there   there

It's the way an elder consoles the hurt child.
There, there, there.

Bringing him close, bringing her close,
into the nexus of an us:

us understanding, us having been there.
There, there. It will get better.

When you're grown, making a living,
I hope you have the chance to do nothing.

To take it in, the medicine of air.
To feel held by the air.

—Charise M. Hoge

YOUR TURN

How can rest sustain your inner spark?

Think about stepping back from constant forward motion. Visualize what this might look like for you. Describe with words or pictures.

What are some choices you can make to recharge your creativity?

Build a plan that supports sustainability. The following menu of self-care is an example.

Menu for Rituals of Self-Care

REST

includes relaxation practices, naps, unplugging

"Rest and be thankful."
William Wordsworth, English poet

REFLECTION

includes journaling, gratitude, imagining

"People who have had little self-reflection live life in a huge reality blind-spot."
Bryant McGill, Simple Reminders

MOVEMENT

includes stretching, yoga, walking, any mindful practice

"All creative activity begins with movement."
Joseph Zinker, Gestalt author

COMMUNION

includes being in nature, being with friends/loved ones, tuning in for inner guidance, prayer

"The beauty of the trees, the softness of the air,
the fragrance of the grass, speaks to me."
Chief Dan George, "My Heart Soars" poem

Meditation fits into every category as it can be rest-based, reflection-based, movement-based, or communion-based.

Be inspired by 'aweness'

Aweness isn't a dictionary word but resonates with the feeling state of awe. To experience that feeling state and let it permeate, give yourself an assignment to contemplate and write down one thing a day that awes you, for ten days.

Day 1

Day 2

Day 3

Day 4

Day 5

Day 6

Day 7

Day 8

Day 9

Day 10

Such an act of contemplation is not like going on a retreat. Rather, amidst your daily routine, you stay keenly attuned to your surroundings. Keep an open channel to muse. Give importance to receptivity and to your inner engagement with the world at hand. More yin for your yang, you could say. When you are in this mode, it is easy to be surprised. The riches of your daily life are sustenance to carry you forward.

Future pull

You can tap into the energy of how you imagine your ideal future. A way to kindle the vibrations of imagination is to use a journaling process with a Pray Rain Journal (see *www.marthabeck.com* author and life coach, who got the idea from Master Coach Jeannette Maw). In her newsletter, Martha explains: "A Pray Rain Journal is basically a written vision board in the form of a small journal. Get yourself a very small empty notebook. Each day write a page as if you were living your ideal life and are journaling about it. Use present tense and write about all the wonderful things that are happening and the ramifications of every event."

Allow the art journal page to inspire your own visioning.

Flow Round and Round in the Creative Cycle

Renewal is a part of the cycle of creativity. Time pulls you forward, but you also inhabit cycles similar to the return of seasons. The writer Jean Giono says, "Days begin and end in the dead of night. They are not shaped long, in the manner of things which lead to ends—arrow, road, man's life on earth. They are shaped round, in the manner of things eternal and stable—sun, world, God." Consider the roundness of your creative leaning, where your endeavors lean and curve and rest on a bend that is always connected to a center where you sit with the Muse.

Four things that disturb your flow

Wherever you find yourself in the creative cycle, you may experience certain challenges. The following four issues may seem like obstacles, but these perspectives can assist your movement forward.

1. Feeling stuck is a threshold

When you are at a standstill, with no flow of ideas, energy, inspiration, or motivation, you feel stuck. It can be a dull and disappointing place. If you sit with it, and allow patience in your relationship with the Muse, something happens. You realize that you are *not stuck*; you are on a threshold. Whatever is beyond that threshold is not apparent—yet. At some point the floodgates will open, and flow will become plentiful.

CHARISE'S TURN

My most recent threshold moment was the other night when a word—not a phrase or sentence, a word—kept orbiting through me to add to a poem I had been working on that day. Struggling to complete a phrase with this one word kept me awake for a couple of hours while lying in bed. Eventually I gave up for the sake of sleep. The next day, still stuck with the word, I meditated. You may think I'm going to tell you that this is where I got inspired, but no, what I got was the understanding that my fingers would figure this out. Once I put my fingers to the keyboard of the computer, the rest of the phrase emerged. The word was a trickle; I had to wait for the flow.

YOUR TURN

Where can you find an opening, a threshold, in a place that feels stuck?

Take a pause…

to allow the Muse to assist you…

out of your standstill.

Be patient…   and receptive.

"In the confrontation between the stream and the rock, the stream always wins, not through strength, but through persistence."
—Buddha

2. A lagging project is sparked by proven success

Find the momentum that underlies an area where you are successful. What is going well for you in one part of your life can kickstart what seems to be lagging. A lagging project can feel like a drain on your energy and can lead to negative ideas about your abilities or thoughts about being a failure. That road is a dead end. However, a stalled endeavor can borrow energy from something that is already going well.

> *"Listen.*
> *Make a way for yourself inside yourself.*
> *Stop looking in the other way of looking.*
> *You already have the precious mixture*
> *that will make you well.*
> *Use it."*
> —Rumi

YOUR TURN

How can you apply the workings of success that you feel in one area toward the makings of another?

Tap into whatever forward-moving energy you have and direct it toward a project you have left idle. Describe how you would leverage this energy.

3. Mistakes are like portals

When you allow yourself to be pulled forward by the energy of a hunch, you learn to incorporate 'mistakes' or 'fortunate accidents' into your creative path. A hunch is like a little nudge—infuse it with curiosity, and it leads you to explore further. Of course, with every new attempt, fear is on the sidelines, distracting your efforts with a suggestion of failure. But this is a method of trial and error. It is like planting seeds: some take root; some sprout, but quickly expire; others seem to grow for a longer time but fade; and still others bear fruit. Statistics tell us that only about one-third of experiments work out. Follow your hunches and use the supposed 'mistakes' as portals to lead you forward in your creative work.

"Errors... are the portals of discovery."
—James Joyce, Ulysses

Maybe

… it was a false start
… an orchestra warming up
… warble seeking wings
… downbeat without a measure
it was never a mistake

—Charise M. Hoge, *Striking Light from Ashes*

YOUR TURN

How can you infuse curiosity into a supposed 'mistake' and use it as a portal?

Return to the impetus of your hunch and imagine other ways it can play out. Sketch out possible scenarios.

4. The dynamic dark offers renewal

In an unexpected dark time, when your efforts are not getting you anywhere, there is another place to go: your inner light. There is a dynamic shift taking place beneath the surface within you.

In the cycle of the seasons, nature offers a renewal period during the winter season. It is sometimes called the 'dead of winter' but, in fact, the hidden forces are teeming with life. In the creativity cycle, your mind wants to keep working on a problem; your body wants to keep trying something different in hopes of a breakthrough or resolution. Sometimes it takes more effort to be still and quiet than to keep circling in the same old pattern. A period of rest takes you deeper, to your creative light within you, so that the images that begin to emerge are from your own spirit of creative expression, and not just something that you make yourself do.

"I need to be silent for a while; worlds are forming in my heart."
—Meister Eckhart, 14th-century German mystic

Mother Nature's cycle allows for a period of rest. As a part of nature, you also get to claim rest in your own cycle of growth. What a challenge it is to be as quiet and still as a snowfall on a winter's night! This period of rest is an experience of being rather than doing. Rest and stillness make a good case for the practice of meditation; it supports the quieting of the mind as well as the body. Your exhalation allows your body to relax into being. There are many ways to be still. Rest in the beauty of your own inner light. No effort needed... rest in your still point.

YOUR TURN

What calls you more deeply toward your inner light as you weather the winter bend of the creative cycle?

For instance, light a candle each evening to remember that your inner light leads you to new growth and expansion. Gaze upon the flame until its essence merges with that light, the essence of creativity within you. Kindle your heart-light.

Name ways that help you rest in your still point.

How can you cultivate faith in your emerging creative expression, to trust the "worlds [that] are forming" in your heart?

Jot down any sparks of inspiration and allow them to gestate during this dynamic dark time of rest. Breathe and allow the silence of renewal to do its magic.

5

BEING
IN RELATIONSHIP
WITH YOUR
CREATIVE NATURE

Acknowledgment ~ Authenticity ~
Affirmation ~ Allow

*"Ensō (circle) is a sacred symbol in the Zen school of
Buddhism and is one of the most common subjects of
Japanese calligraphy... [Ancient texts refer] to the way of Zen
as a 'circle of vast space, lacking nothing and holding nothing
in excess'. At first glance the ancient ensō symbol appears to
be nothing more than a miss-shaped circle but its symbolism
refers to the beginning and end of all things, the circle of life
and the connectedness of existence... Ensō can be the open
circle of emptiness in which the self flows in and out while
remaining centered; leaving the ensō open is like leaving
room for the spirit to flow in and out of the
circle of emptiness."*
—modernzen.org

The ensō is a fitting image for the last chapter highlighting creative nature. You come round full circle, as your creative nature expresses the essence of being, highlighted in the first chapter. You embody the essence, express it, circling in its flow, through your unique expression. What seems like an ending is in fact another beginning.

KATE'S TURN

I took a class to learn about the ensō, and to learn how to paint it. I found it very challenging to set intention, load the brush with enough India ink to complete the calligraphy, and, with only one gesture, place ink to the rice paper and create an open circle, lifting the brush just before completing the circle. I had to remain centered and focused while open to the process. I find this concept even more challenging to live: staying grounded and centered in my being while being open and responsive to external factors. This represents an aspect of the nature of my previous work as a psychologist, facilitating people to anchor deeply within themselves while navigating circumstances in their lives. Staying connected to oneself and to all that is results in being fully engaged in the circle of life.

"When you believe that you have arrived at some final destination on your path, ensō reminds you to start again exactly at the point where you are now and to embrace and enjoy your unique experiences on life's journey."
—modernzen.org

Acknowledgment

You are born creative. The creative impulse is hardwired in you as part of your true nature. Your creative capacity may lie dormant, like a flicker of light, a spark of divinity. And this eternal flame, by virtue of the fact that you are alive, will never go out.

> "We are intended to create… [We are] in alignment with our true nature when we create."
> —Julia Cameron, *The Artist's Way*

Sometimes life events preclude creative work or play. Circumstances may compromise your ability to express creatively. Plans for projects or endeavors are put on hold, derailed, interrupted—from the way you expected them to happen. Even so, there continues to be your underlying current of creativity that you are drawing upon. Your innate creative nature helps you to manage your circumstances and supports your creative expression. You can trust your flow. Consider ebb and flow: when a tide ebbs, you know that it will flow again. Flow isn't something to force; it's natural. Keep a quiet witnessing of your creative tide. It will surprise you.

> "Your soul knows the geography of your destiny. Your soul alone has the map of your future; therefore, you can trust this indirect, oblique side of yourself. If you do, it will take you where you need to go, but more important it will teach you a kindness of rhythm in your journey."
> —John O'Donohue, *Anam Cara: A Book of Celtic Wisdom*

YOUR TURN

How are you kindling your creative spark within?

Pay attention to your sources of inspiration—nature, exhibits, events, conversations, technology—and seek them out. Make a list.

*In what ways can you acknowledge your creative
nature as the simple outpouring of your life?*

Name the ways you infuse creativity into the rhythm of your
life. Some examples are parenting, cooking, problem-solving.

Authenticity

The force that opens the blooms and guides the stars also guides you. Flowers blossom by their very nature. You are an exquisite expression of nature. You are creating all the time. What's more, you can't help it—you are just being yourself.

> *"The flower doesn't dream of the bee; it blossoms…*
> *and the bee comes."*
> —Mark Nepo, *The Book of Awakening*

Your most natural expression of your creativity comes out of who you are. Simply and profoundly, be your authentic self. A mosaic of creative expressions will flow with ease.

On The Porch

"He who kisses the joy as it flies."—William Blake

August.
At the behest
of nature, life feels epiphanous.

In the simultaneous
lazy, longevity grows slender
Thick with humid blooms, summer's

bound to shift. I swoon over
this butterfly—suddenly my worst fear
lacks reason to exist—
as it lights upon these sighing lips.

—Charise M. Hoge, *Muse in a Suitcase*

YOUR TURN

How do you access your voice?

Notice how you are already doing this in your life. Are you reflecting, journaling, drawing, engaging in movement, dialogue, or other exploratory resources? Note the ways.

"That inner voice has both gentleness and clarity. So to get to authenticity, you really keep going down to the bone, to the honesty, and the inevitability of something."
—Meredith Monk, performing artist

Affirmation

Your unique expression is an affirmation of the essential energy within you. Your creative nature embodies this abundant energy that you express throughout your life. Your creative practice *becomes* your life.

Think of the stitches that together make a tapestry, and how each separate stitch contributes to the overall look and feel of the whole. The tapestry is too large to see in its entirety, and it is continually in the making. Stay with this image. You may find that you are in awe of the magnitude and uniqueness of the tapestry that is your life.

Feel the immensity of what you are experiencing. Be wowed. Give thanks that you are part of a greater mystery, the 'co' of co-create. You can experience gratitude as a qualitative state, something like reverence. It is not really about selecting what you are grateful for; it is about expanding your view toward a holistic gratitude.

"Gratitude is the most passionate transformative
force in the cosmos."
—Sarah Ban Breathnach, *The Simple Abundance Journal of Gratitude*

YOUR TURN

How does your life reflect an affirmation of your creative nature?

Step back and visualize the 'tapestry that is your life,' taking it all in with a spirit of gratitude. Note your reflections.

Allow

Your life honors the abundance that never ceases by virtue of your creative nature. Allow your entire life to be a blessing. You are a maker, a creator, a blessing. Be the blessing.

> *"I am in the Universe.*
> *The Universe is in my body.*
> *The Universe and I combine together."*
> —Master Chunyi Lin

And so, you have come full circle.

Like the ensō, remain open to continue the creative journey in relationship with your Muse.

NOTES

BIBLIOGRAPHY

Cameron, Julia. *The Artist's Way*. New York: Penguin Putman Inc, 1992.

Hoge, Charise. *Muse in a Suitcase*. American Fork, Utah: Kelsay Books, 2021.

Hoge, Charise. *Striking Light from Ashes*. Georgetown, Kentucky: Finishing Line Press, 2017.

Lao Tzu. *Tao Te Ching*. Chinese Classic Text, 400 BCE.

Tolle, Eckhart. *A New Earth*. New York: Penguin Group, 2005.

RESOURCES

www.authentichappiness.sas.upenn.edu/testcenter

www.charisehoge.com

www.cloudappreciationsociety.org

www.kroskalifecoaching.com

www.marthabeck.com

www.meetyourmuseblog.com

www.springforestqigong.com

ABOUT THE AUTHORS

Charise M. Hoge, MA, MSW, is a dance/movement therapist, writer, life coach, and performing artist. Her work in the healing arts includes programs for hospitals, counseling centers, businesses, the Smithsonian's National Zoo, the United States Holocaust Memorial Museum, and the World Bank. A yoga practitioner for twenty-five years, she integrates SynergyDance principles and yoga mudras in her teaching. Based on her experience living and working abroad, Charise co-authored a different kind of travel guide titled *A Portable Identity: A Woman's Guide to Maintaining a Sense of Self While Moving Overseas* (new edition forthcoming). Her poetry is featured in various literary journals, the book *Next Line, Please: Prompts to Inspire Poets and Writers*, as well as her chapbooks *Striking Light from Ashes* and *Muse in a Suitcase*.

Kathleen M. Kroska, MA, has worked in the health field as a licensed psychologist, having specialized in holistic care and energy psychology. She is certified as a life coach, with specialties in health and creativity. Kate received training in qigong and has been a qigong instructor. All these disciplines have been integrated in her professional work. Her most recent creative expression is watercolor, which she learned while living on her sailboat in the Caribbean. There she had two solo exhibits, weaving spirituality and healing into her arts. Kate has coauthored the *Meet Your Muse* blog for over twelve years; this publication distills the best of those writings. She currently lives in St. Paul, MN.

Printed in the USA
CPSIA information can be obtained
at www.ICGtesting.com
CBHW040830090424
6604CB00011B/58

9 781915 548160